Past and Present
SHIPS

Neil Morris

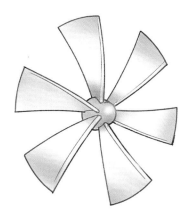

 Belitha Press

First published in the UK in 1999 by
Belitha Press Limited,
London House, Great Eastern Wharf,
Parkgate Road, London SW11 4NQ

Copyright © Belitha Press Limited 1999
Text copyright © Neil Morris 1999
First published with higher text level as *Travelling Through Time: Ships* in 1997

ISBN 1 85561 894 X

British Library Cataloguing in Publication Data
for this book is available from the British Library

Printed in Hong Kong

Editor: Honor Head
Designer: Helen James
Picture researcher: Juliet Duff

25692607

Words in **bold** appear in the glossary on pages 30–31

Picture acknowledgements:
t=top; b=bottom; c=centre; r=right l=left

AA & A: 16 both
J. Allan Cash: 28c
Bridgeman Art Library: 17
Mary Evans Picture Library: 13r, 25l
Robert Harding Picture Library 8l, 9, 12t, 13l, 20t
Michael Holford: 8r, 21
Hulton Getty Picture Collection: 12b
Peter Newark's Pictures: 20b, 24t
Fred Olsen Travel: 29t
Princess Cruises: 28–29b
Quadrant Picture Library: 28t
Retrograph Archive Ltd: 4–5t, 24b
Stena Line: 5b
Tony Stone Worldwide: 4b, 25r

Front cover and main artworks by Terry Hadler
All other artworks by Graham Rosewarne

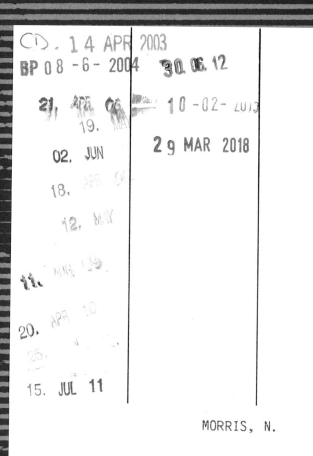

Contents

Introduction

Ships are the oldest form of long-distance transport. They have carried people and goods for at least 5000 years. Large ships sail the world's oceans, while smaller boats make shorter voyages on lakes and rivers.

▲ Fun and games on the deck of a 1920s ocean liner.

◄ Chinese **junks** are still used as working ships and to carry tourists.

Sailing ships

Early boats and ships were made of reeds and then planks of wood. They were rowed with oars. Then sails were used to help move them. Sailing ships grew in size until they reached their biggest in the mid-1800s.

Changing times

Steamships were launched in the nineteenth century. They were made of iron instead of wood. Today, large **ferries**, are popular and huge **cargo** ships are as busy as ever.

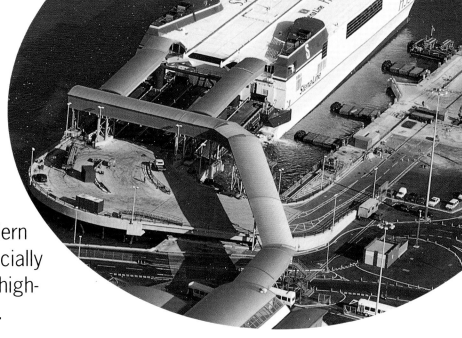

► Some modern ports are specially designed for high-speed ferries.

Trading by sea

In ancient times, ships were used to explore new lands and to trade with other people. Ships were also important in wartime. They carried fighting men and weapons to enemy shores.

This Roman **merchant ship** sailed in AD 200. Ships like this carried a wide range of cargo.

Ancient sailors

The ancient Egyptians made boats from bundles of reeds. Then, about 5000 years ago they discovered that boats could be moved along by sails that caught the wind. Later, they made ships from wood. The Phoenicians, from the eastern Mediterranean coast, built fast fighting ships. The ancient Greeks used a similar design, and by 300 BC their biggest ships had four sails.

Merchant ships

The Romans built up the largest sailing **fleet** of ancient times, and their merchant ships were over 50 metres long. At that time there were no real passenger ships. Travellers had to sail on merchant ships, and they often shared the small cabins with slaves and prisoners.

▼ This wooden boat was found in a pit beside the Great Pyramid in Egypt. It may have been used to carry a **pharaoh's** body across the River Nile.

▲ This picture was found on the wall of an Egyptian tomb. It shows the mayor of Thebes and his wife sailing on the Nile around 1450 BC. Thebes was once the capital of Egypt.

▼ About 3000 years ago, the Phoenicians sailed all over the Mediterranean and beyond to trade with other countries.

Spain

Italy

Greece

Sidon

Carthage

Tyre

Mediterranean Sea

Alexandria

Egypt

Phoenicia
Phoenician trading areas

North Africa

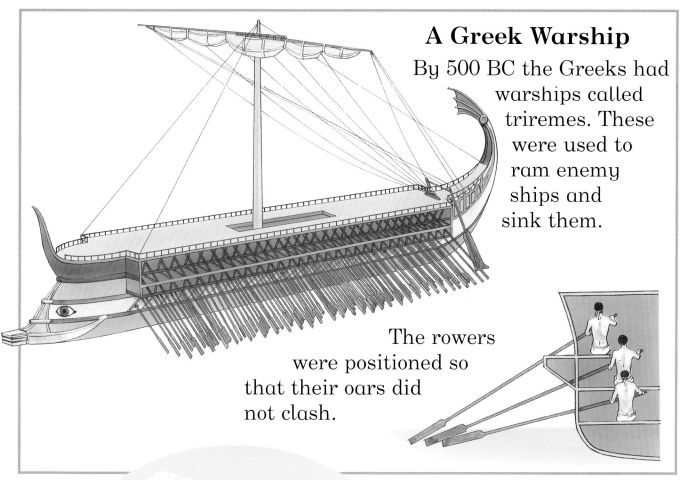

A Greek Warship

By 500 BC the Greeks had warships called triremes. These were used to ram enemy ships and sink them.

The rowers were positioned so that their oars did not clash.

◀ This man is rowing his reed boat on Lake Titicaca in the Andes mountains, between Peru and Bolivia in South America. The boat is made from reeds that grow by the shores of the lake.

Crossing oceans

Nobody knows exactly when people first sailed across the world's two biggest oceans, the Pacific and the Atlantic. But it is certain that they travelled in all sorts of ships, from simple rafts to fast longships.

A Viking **longship** had a sail made of tough woollen cloth and strips of leather.

Canoes and rafts

The original Polynesian islanders of the south Pacific probably sailed there from south-east Asia between 1000 and 3000 years ago. They travelled in large canoes, using sails and paddles. Others may have sailed on **balsa-wood rafts**.

Viking voyages

The Vikings used their longships to raid other people's lands. The ships had up to 30 oars on each side, but on the open sea a sail was used. About the year 1000, a Viking called Leif Eriksson sailed to present-day Canada and north-east USA. This great voyage took place nearly 500 years before Christopher Columbus crossed the Atlantic.

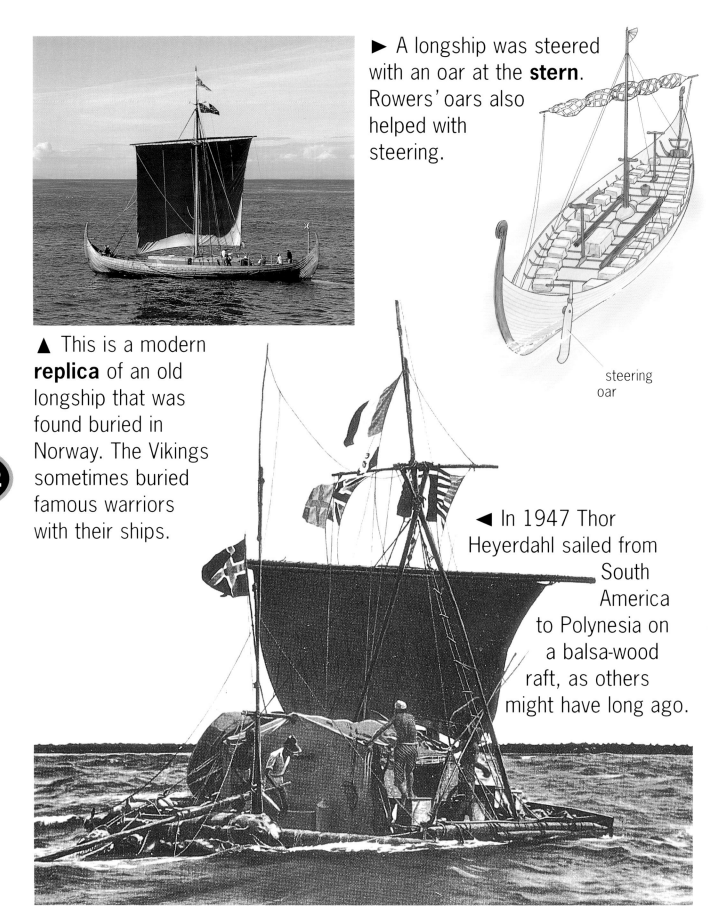

► A longship was steered with an oar at the **stern**. Rowers' oars also helped with steering.

steering oar

▲ This is a modern **replica** of an old longship that was found buried in Norway. The Vikings sometimes buried famous warriors with their ships.

◄ In 1947 Thor Heyerdahl sailed from South America to Polynesia on a balsa-wood raft, as others might have long ago.

▼ This ship is called a dhow. It was originally an Arab ship. Dhows have sailed for many centuries in the Persian Gulf and the Red Sea. The sail runs along the length of the ship rather than across it.

▲ The people of the Solomon Islands, in the Pacific Ocean, used to go to sea in huge wooden canoes. Today the canoes are mostly used for special ceremonies.

Clinker-built ships have planks that overlap each other. Carvel-built ships have planks next to each other.

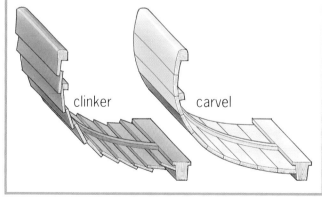

clinker   carvel

Sailing to America

By about 1250, shipbuilders in Europe were making strong trading ships. They had a wide hull and a new method of steering using a rudder.

The *Mayflower* was 27 metres long. It had three masts and a **bowsprit** at the **prow.** These gave a total of six sails.

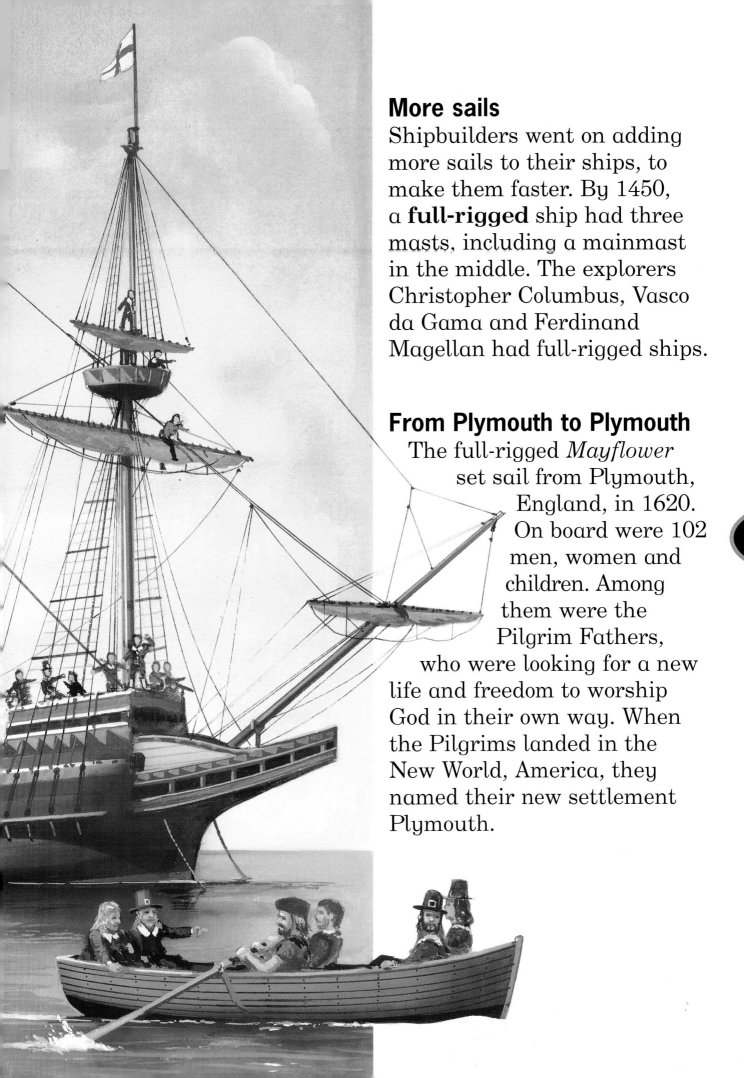

More sails

Shipbuilders went on adding more sails to their ships, to make them faster. By 1450, a **full-rigged** ship had three masts, including a mainmast in the middle. The explorers Christopher Columbus, Vasco da Gama and Ferdinand Magellan had full-rigged ships.

From Plymouth to Plymouth

The full-rigged *Mayflower* set sail from Plymouth, England, in 1620. On board were 102 men, women and children. Among them were the Pilgrim Fathers, who were looking for a new life and freedom to worship God in their own way. When the Pilgrims landed in the New World, America, they named their new settlement Plymouth.

Inside the *Mayflower*

1 Forecastle, where the crew slept and ate.
2 Windlass, a machine for raising the anchor.
3 Hold, the main cargo area.
4 Capstan, a pulley used to pull up cargo.
5 Cabin for the ship's officers.

6 Whipstaff, a lever that moved the rudder.
7 Chart-room, where maps were studied.
8 Captain's cabin.
9 Passengers' quarters.
10 Gun room, with two cannon.

▲ This thirteenth-century trading ship was called a cog. The large **sterncastle** at the back sheltered the passengers and crew.

▼ A replica of the *Santa Maria*. This was one of the three ships which took Columbus to the New World in 1492.

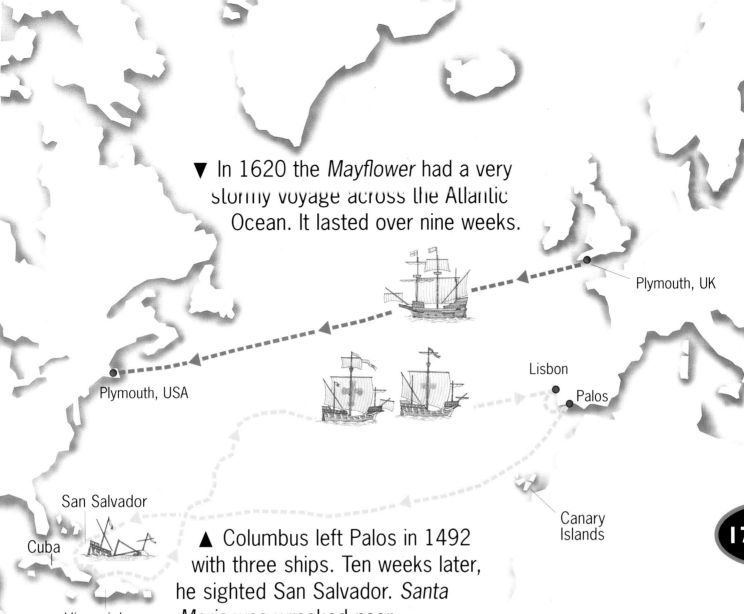

▼ In 1620 the *Mayflower* had a very stormy voyage across the Atlantic Ocean. It lasted over nine weeks.

Plymouth, UK

Plymouth, USA

Lisbon

Palos

San Salvador

Cuba

Hispaniola

Canary Islands

▲ Columbus left Palos in 1492 with three ships. Ten weeks later, he sighted San Salvador. *Santa Maria* was wrecked near Hispaniola, so only two ships returned to Spain in 1493.

◄ The clipper, *Flying Cloud*, was built in 1851. Clippers got their name because their speed allowed them to clip days off normal sailing times.

17

Full steam ahead

For thousands of years ships were powered by the wind or by human energy. The invention of the steam engine in the late eighteenth century changed things. But the first steamships still had sails, in case the engine broke down!

The *Great Eastern*, launched in 1858, had a **propeller, paddle wheels** and sails.

Early steamships

The first successful steamship was built in America in 1807. Twelve years later, the American-built *Savannah* became the first steamship to cross the Atlantic to Europe. By 1835 paddle-steamers were making regular crossings.

Brunel's big ships

The British engineer Isambard Kingdom Brunel launched his steamship *Great Britain* in 1843. Then came *Great Eastern*, which was 211 metres long and could carry 4000 passengers. This was easily the largest ship built up to that time. It was later used to lay a telegraph cable across the Atlantic.

19

▲ This is a modern example of a Mississippi River steamer. This type of ship is driven by one large paddle wheel.

propeller

◄ The Suez Canal opened in 1869. It links the Mediterranean Sea with the Red Sea.

The design of ships' propellers has changed over the years.

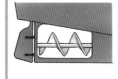

an early screw propeller

bladed propeller

Great Britain's propeller

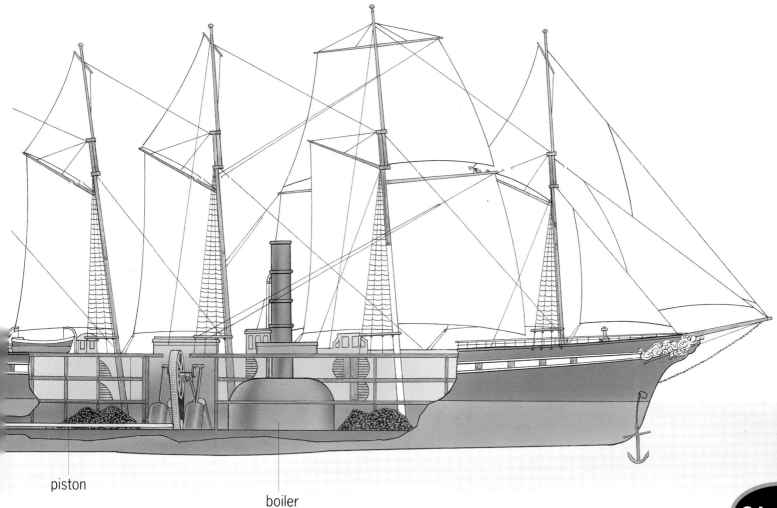

piston

boiler

▲ In a steamship like *Great Britain*, coal was burned to make steam in the boiler. The steam pushed pistons which turned a long shaft. The shaft turned the propeller, which pushed the ship along.

▲ The *Savannah* arrives at Liverpool in 1819, after crossing the Atlantic Ocean in 29 days.

The Blue Riband

The great ocean liners of the twentieth century were among the most famous and best-loved ships of all time. The fastest liners competed for a very special trophy.

The *Queen Mary* was 310 metres long – half as long again as the *Great Eastern*. It first crossed the Atlantic in 1936.

Transatlantic trophy

The award for the fastest Atlantic crossing was called the Bluc Riband. The *Queen Mary* crossed the Atlantic a couple of times before it came up to full speed. Then it won the award by steaming from New York to Southampton in under four days. In 1952 the American **liner** *United States* set a new record of three and a half days.

Travelling in luxury

Passengers travelled in luxury on these huge ocean liners. They were like floating hotels, with ballrooms, swimming pools and sports courts. But during the 1950s and 1960s the liners had to compete with jet aircraft. The planes were not so luxurious, but they were faster.

► The *Titanic* sank on its first voyage, in 1912. It struck an iceberg in the north Atlantic,and 1500 people died. The tragedy led to new safety regulations and more lifeboats.

▼ The French liner *Normandie* competed for size, speed and luxury with the British ships *Queen Mary* and *Queen Elizabeth*.

▼ The *QE2* was launched in 1967. It still cruises all over the world.

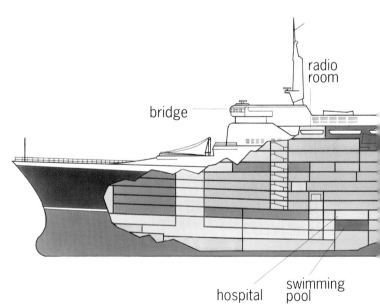

▼ The *Queen Mary* is now a luxury hotel and tourist attraction in Long Beach, California. The liner was taken out of service in 1967.

▲ One of the *Queen Mary's* luxury, first-class cabins.

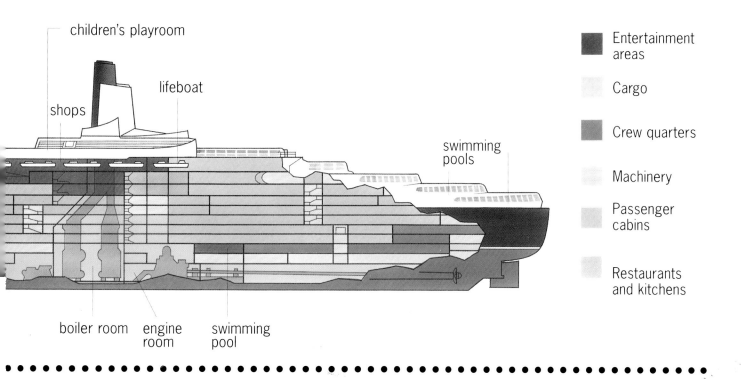

children's playroom

lifeboat

shops

swimming pools

boiler room

engine room

swimming pool

Entertainment areas

Cargo

Crew quarters

Machinery

Passenger cabins

Restaurants and kitchens

Speeding into the future

Car and passenger ferries have been in use for many years. Ferries are now getting bigger and faster, as they try to compete with planes for passengers.

This HSS (High-speed Sea Service) ferry carries 1500 passengers and 375 cars. It is 124 metres long and 40 metres wide.

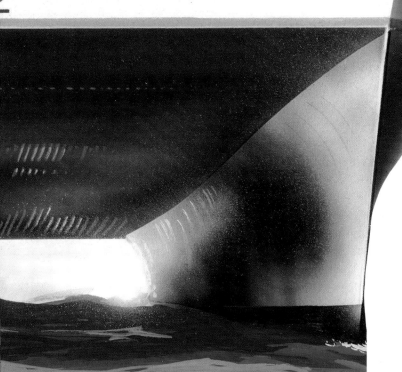

High-speed ferries

Some new fast ferries have two **hulls**. They do not roll from side to side as much as other ships and are more comfortable for passengers. HSS ferries are powered by four jet engines. Movable nozzles turn the jets and steer the ship.

All kinds of craft

Today, most big liners are used for holiday cruises. Liners and ferries are getting bigger and faster, but the world's biggest ships are oil tankers. Ships have been travelling the world's seas for thousands of years, and new ships and boats will go on doing so in the future.

Hydrofoil

At high speeds a **hydrofoil** lifts up onto wings, called foils. This makes it skim across the water and go faster.

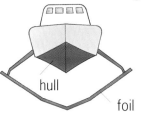

hull

foil

floating on its hull

speeding on its foils

◄ This luxury private cruiser has its own helicopter on board. Such big ships are very expensive to run.

▼ Cars and lorries drive through the loading gates of an HSS ferry.

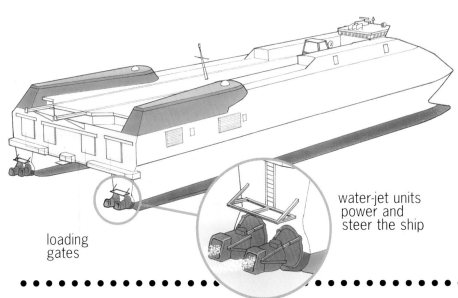

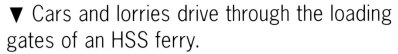

loading gates

water-jet units power and steer the ship

► This modern clipper carries holidaymakers to the Indian Ocean and the Caribbean. A crew of 72 looks after 170 passengers.

▼ *Sun Princess* offers the latest in luxury cruising. It is 261 metres long and can carry nearly 2000 passengers.

Glossary

balsa-wood A very light type of wood that comes from tropical trees of Central and South America.

bowsprit A pole that points forwards from the front of a ship and which can carry a sail.

cargo Goods carried on a ship.

ferry A ship that carries passengers, cars and goods.

fleet A number of ships belonging to one nation.

full-rigged Having three or more masts.

hull The main body of a ship.

hydrofoil A boat that can lift itself onto wings so that it skims across the water at high speed.

junk A Chinese sailing ship with square sails supported by bamboo rods.

liner A large ship that regularly carries passengers on a long voyage.

longship A long, narrow Viking ship with oars and a square sail.

merchant ship A trading ship used for carrying goods.

paddle wheel A large wheel with boards that push against the water to drive the ship along.

pharaoh An ancient Egyptian ruler.

propeller A set of blades that turn in the water to push a ship along.

prow The front end of a ship.

raft A flat wooden boat, often made of logs tied together.

replica An exact copy.

steamship A ship that is powered by a steam engine.

stern The back end of a ship.

sterncastle A raised structure at the back of a ship.

Index

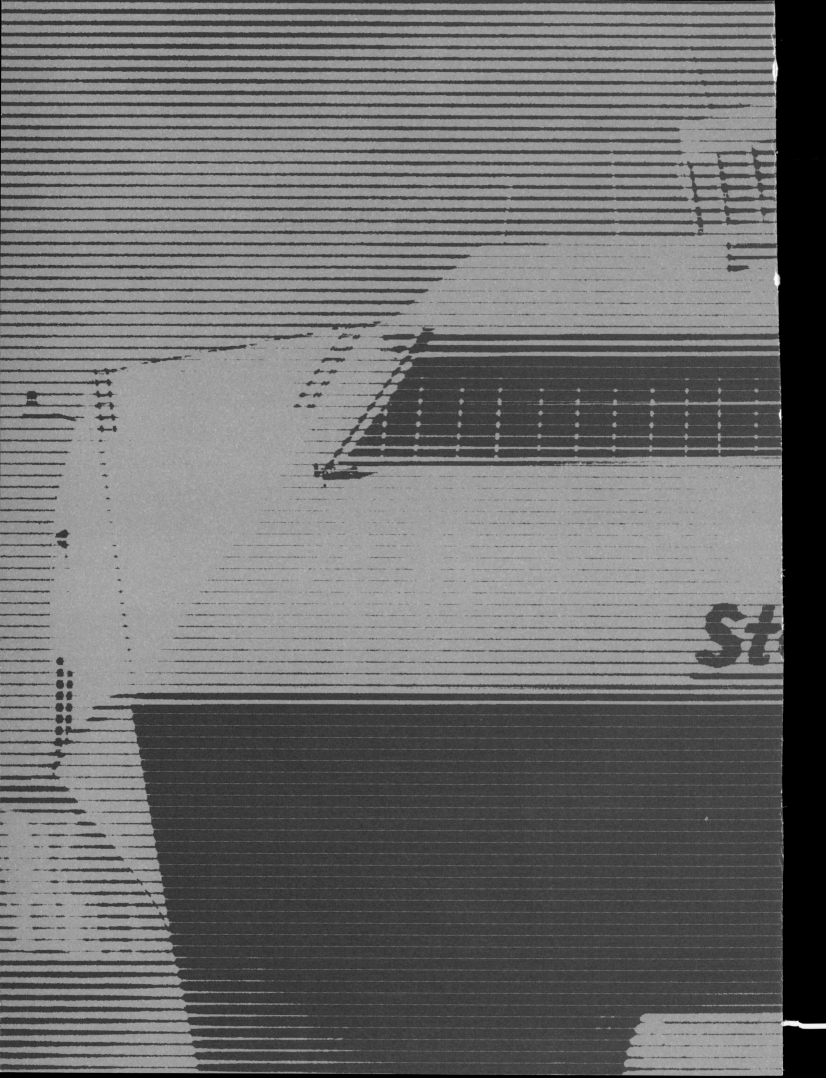